DESIGNING THE FUTURE

Published by Creative Education
123 South Broad Street, Mankato, Minnesota 56001
Creative Education is an imprint of The Creative Company

Designed by Stephanie Blumenthal
Editorial Assistance by Adele Richardson

Photographs by Michelle Burgess, Richard Cummins, Don Eastman,
Priscilla Alexander Eastman, Herbert L. Gatewood, Beryl Goldberg, Richard T. Nowitz,
Root Resources, Eugene G. Schulz, and Tom Stack & Associates

Library of Congress Cataloging-in-Publication Data

Willard, Keith.
Bridges / by Keith Willard
p. cm. — (Designing the future)
Includes index
Summary: Examines the history, design, construction, and uses of bridges
and describes some notable examples.
ISBN 0-88682-718-3
1. Bridges—Juvenile literature. [1. Bridges.] I. Title. II. Series.
TG148.W54   1999
624'.2—dc21   98-17173

4   6   8   9   7   5   3

DESIGNING THE FUTURE

BRIDGES

KEITH WILLARD

CREATIVE EDUCATION

As the construction crew put the finishing touches on the Akashi Kaikyo Bridge, they felt a great sense of pride. After 10 years of construction, the final link between the southern island and northern island of Japan was complete. This massive man-made structure would stand as the longest bridge in the world . . . at least for awhile. Work is constantly being done to design and construct longer, bigger bridges. Among mankind's most impressive structures, bridges range in length from a few feet (meters) to many miles

Broadway Bridge at Saskatoon

Natural Bridge in Virginia

(kilometers) long. Depending on the technology of the builder, bridges can be made of wood, stone, steel, or even vines—whatever it takes to shorten the distance between two points.

The first man-made bridge was probably a copy of something found in nature. In the north, freezing temperatures can turn small lakes and ponds to ice, creating a natural bridge. Rivers may have shallow areas where large rocks and boulders stick out above

N A M I N G

Condemned prisoners once padded over the Bridge of Sighs, a covered bridge in Venice, Italy on their way from the judgement hall to the place of execution.

Great Smoky Mountains National Park

Rainbow Bridge National Monument in Utah

the water, creating a natural walkway. Large tree roots and vines snake over small ravines to form unique bridges. Other bridges found in nature are made of rock. One example is the Natural Bridge in Virginia. It was formed over millions of years by running water wearing away at solid rock.

Some of the bridges found in nature are extremely old and delicate. They may have survived

The Tarr Steps in England is the oldest known bridge in the world. It's made of piles of rocks with stone slabs on top. Historians believe it to be over 10,000 years old.

hundreds, even thousands of years against the forces of time and nature. Many stand as monuments of what nature can do without any help from people and advancing technology.

Thousands of years ago, someone needed to cross a stream. That person probably took a log or a fallen tree and placed it over the running water to get to the other side, creating a beam bridge. If a stream

Bridge near Dundee, Scotland

was wider than one fallen tree could span, a pier was made in the middle of the stream by standing a log upright and laying the trees over it that reached to either bank. The weight of the beam presses straight down and is supported by the land on either side and the pier, if there is one. To make a beam bridge stronger, truss work or girders may be added to it. These are often built into a frame-

The Trajans Bridge crossed the Danube river in Romania. It had 21 arches, stretched over 3,000 feet (914 m), and contained well over 1 million stones, each weighing over half a ton (450 kg). Rome's own legions destroyed it 150 years later while retreating from battle.

work of triangular shapes to spread out the support evenly.

Some of the oldest surviving bridges in the world are made of stone. Several can be found in Europe. These bridges are simple beam designs with heavy slabs of stone forming the walkway. They are called clam or clapper bridges. The clam bridge is made of a single stone slab resting on the ground at

Pont du Gard in France

Samur-en-Auxois at Burgundy, France

Longest covered bridge in Quebec, Canada

each end. The clapper was built to cover a longer distance. More than one stone slab was used with rocks and stones piled up in the middle, forming the piers. No one knows for certain how old these types of durable bridges are, but many historians estimate their age to be several thousand years.

The arch bridge design tends to survive because the weight of it does not press straight down as it does with a beam bridge. Instead, the weight is carried outward and is distributed through the curve, pressing into the abutments. An arch bridge is built around a temporary frame that holds all the pieces in place. When the last piece, called the keystone, is wedged into place, the framework is removed and the bridge is complete. Once the last piece is in position, all the stones press against each other to stay in place.

The strength and longevity of many arch bridges is attributed not only to the design of the arch, but also to the use of pozzolana, a type of lasting cement made from volcanic clay. This clay is found in great quantities in east-central Italy. Unlike other cements, it could be made into mortar that was used under water without disintegrating, and it hardened to

In 1874, the first all-steel bridge was built in the U.S. The Eads Bridge is a triple-arch in St. Louis, Missouri, that spans the width of the Mississippi River.

the density of the stone itself.

Bridges made by ancient Romans are some of the most beautiful structures in the world. They discovered that if a river or chasm was too wide for a single arch design, a bridge of several arches could be built to close the gap. The famous Pons Aelius Bridge completed in 134 A.D. has seven arches. It still stands

Lethbridge in Alberta, Canada—the world's longest train bridge

today, over 1,800 years later. In fact, the largest majority of modern bridges made from steel or concrete still use the arch principle in their construction.

While many stone bridges have stood the test of time, wooden bridges are becoming increasingly rare. There are many rea-

In 1997, the first plastic bridge was built in Grafton, West Virginia. Not only does it resist corrosion (rust), it is expected to last three times longer than bridges made of concrete and steel.

sons for this. Wood is not as strong as stone, and it deteriorates when left exposed to natural elements. Insects can also eat away at the wood, leaving the bridge weak and dangerous.

Covered bridges are one interesting type of wooden bridge quickly becoming scarce. Barn-like buildings

Ponte Scaligero and Castel Vechhio in Verona, Italy

Old North Bridge in Concord, Massachusetts

were constructed over the bridges to help protect them from snow, rain, and early deterioration. Most covered bridges found in the United States are over 150 years old and are kept in repair for historical reasons rather than for regular use.

Oddly enough, nearly all early bridges built for railroads in Europe, Canada, and the United States were made of wood. Although most were strong enough to carry the weight of the heavy engines and loaded freight cars, many people were afraid to cross them. A train would have to stop, unload passengers, and let them walk across after the train was safely on the other side.

During the 19th century, iron began to replace wood. It was far

The Colossus Bridge was completed in 1812 over the Schuylkill River in Pennsylvania. Made of wood, it spanned 340 feet (104 m), and was painted white to make it visible for miles. Fire destroyed it in 1838.

stronger, not subject to fire, and would last much longer with less maintenance. The spans grew larger with each new design. But even with this new and stronger material there were still a large number of bridge failures. As the trains and rail cars became heavier, many bridges collapsed under their burden. Fortunately, a new metal, called steel, was developed during this same time. This proved to be a safer, stronger metal for bridge building.

Scotland's first all steel bridge, the Firth of Forth,

Firth of Forth railroad bridge in Edinburgh, Scotland

was built in 1890. This cantilever bridge stretches more than a mile and a half (1.8 km) long, and was built with more than 59,000 tons (53,690 MT) of steel. A bridge of this design is balanced on heavy piers with arms (cantilevers) reaching out to connect with the arms of the structure next to it. The Firth of Forth has three cantilever sections and two spans connecting it to shore. For additional sup-

In 1940, the Tacoma Narrows Bridge collapsed during high winds in Washington State. This disaster led to the redesigning of suspension bridge decks so that air flows more safely around them.

port, steel truss work was woven into the cantilevers. This bridge is so sturdy that it still carries high speed railway traffic today. Steel can be found in most of today's bridges. Even modern bridges that look like stone are actually made of reinforced concrete. The cables of suspension bridges are made of steel wires, and today's arch bridges are made of steel or a concrete and steel mixture. Australia's

Sydney Harbor Bridge in Australia

Hoffstadt Canyon Bridge in Washington

Sydney Harbor Bridge is a wonderful example of a steel arch bridge. It opened in 1932, and spans 1,650 feet (503 m). Unlike most arch bridges where the roadway runs on top, Sydney Harbor has its decking suspended below the arch by cables.

While most people think of bridges as fixed structures used to get from one point to another, there are many bridges built specifically to be movable. These are often constructed when a high bridge is not practical, or is too expensive.

The most well-known of the movable designs are bascule bridges, otherwise known as drawbridges. Bascule is a French word that means "seesaw," which is very much how the bridge operates. A roadway (the

In 1967, the London Bridge was sold to a private developer, who dismantled it and brought it to the U.S. There it was perfectly reerected in the Arizona desert.

London's Tower Bridge

Lift bridges in Ohio (above) and Washington (below)

ers. Each section of the double-leaf bascule weighs over 1,200 pounds (540 kg), but powerful motors can lift them in four minutes. A vertical lift bridge is similar to an elevator. The decking is not hinged, but attached to two towers at each end. When a ship approaches, cables in each of the towers lift the span straight up so the ship can pass through.

A swing bridge does not move up or down, but turns from side to side. The span is usually balanced at

bascule) is hinged at one end and can be lifted up by counterweights or hydraulic machinery. A bascule bridge can be single-leaf, such as the drawbridge over the moat at a medieval castle, or double-leaf where two sections of roadway rise at the same time. London's Tower Bridge is one of the best known bascule bridges. This bridge opened in 1894, and is very attractive with its gothic spires set atop two high tow-

Mackinaw Bridge, Michigan

the center and set on a pier. On the pier are wheels that spin the decking so ships can move through. Once they are past, the roadway swings back into position and traffic can resume. A rare movable design is the transporter bridge. A steel frame holds cables attached to a cage that drivers pull into. Once secured, the cage ferries its passengers across water, looking much like a cable car. One of these bridges, the Rendsberg Bridge, can be found in Germany over the Kiel Canal. Usually a bridge of this design is built where road traffic is light and water traffic is heavy.

Before a bridge is built, engineers must take into consideration what type is needed. Generally, suspension bridges can cover much larger spans than

The Humber Bridge in England was beginning to rust from the inside in 1992. To solve the problem engineers used chemicals that absorb moisture, and a machine that dries air like a huge hair dryer.

either the beam or arch designs. The deck, or roadway, of this type of bridge is suspended in the air by huge cables which are draped over tall towers and anchored at the ends on shore. Usually there are two towers. Some of the weight of the bridge

Brooklyn Bridge in New York

is carried along the cables and up to the towers which partially absorb the burden, although most of the weight is transferred further down to the ground on either shore.

The cables of early suspension bridges were iron chains, but today they are made of thousands of steel wires that are twisted and bound together. The two main cables are what run over the towers. Attached to them are vertical cables that connect to the

Lion's Gate Bridge in Vancouver, British Columbia

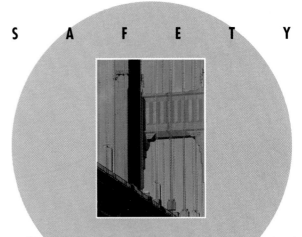

S A F E T Y

Hardhats were first invented for use on San Francisco's Golden Gate Bridge.

roadway. The newest type of suspension bridge is the cable-stayed bridge. This design was developed by German engineers in the 1950s. It is similar to a suspension bridge except that the cables are connected directly to the towers for support, instead of draped over them. To begin constructing a bridge of this magnitude, huge caissons, or concrete tubes, are sunk into the riverbed until they reach solid rock. The water and sand are pumped out and filled with concrete to form the base of a tall tower. After the towers are built, the main cables are spun and set in place; then the roadway is built. Often it is put together in sections and hoisted into place, where it can be attached to the main cables by smaller vertical ones.

Because of their design, suspension bridges can span a vast distance of water; some are more than a

Chesapeake Bay Bridge and tunnel in Virginia

mile (kilometer) in length. The Golden Gate Bridge in San Francisco, California, was completed in 1937. It reigned as the longest bridge in the world at 4,200 feet (1280 m) until 1964 when it was surpassed by the Verrazano-Narrows Bridge in New York, which carries a double deck roadway for 12 lanes of traffic. Its steel towers are 680 feet (207 m) high. The four main suspension cables are three feet (1 m) in diameter and contain enough wire to circle the globe nearly six times. This is still the longest suspension bridge in the United

Brooklyn Bridge in New York

States, but there are several around the world that are even greater.

In 1981, the Humber Bridge near Hull, England, became the world's longest span at 4,626 feet (1,410 m). During the 1990s, two bridges in China were built to be even longer; and

The oldest known single-arch bridge is in Turkey. Spanning the Meles River, this construction wonder is believed by historians to be nearly 3000 years old.

in Denmark, the Great Belt Bridge held the title momentarily at 5,328 feet (1,624 m). The Akashi Kaikyo Bridge across Osaka Bay in northern Japan opened in April 1998. Work on the bridge began in 1988, and, with a total length of 12,828 feet (3,910 m), it is the final link in a chain of six other suspension bridges connecting the southern island of Japan with

Ponti S. Angelo over the Tiber River in Italy

the northern island. Including viaducts on the islands, the entire bridge structure (called the Great Seto) has a total roadway of eight miles (13 km).

An even greater combination bridge is the Chesapeake Bay Bridge in Virginia that spans a total length of over 17 miles (27 km). It is constructed with sections of beam, suspension, cantilever,

The Pontchartrain Causeway in Louisiana is built with hundreds of concrete spans. At 20 miles (32km) in length, this structure is so great that, from the center of the bridge, the land on either end is not visible.

and two tunnels that actually go under water. Bridges, both natural and man-made, are pathways that allow us to get from one place to another. They save us time, and certainly make it easier for vehicles to cross over water. However, not all bridges are meant to cross water. Some have been constructed

Tarrytown Tappan Zee Bridge over the Hudson River, New York

over valleys or swamps where a road would be impossible to build. Other bridges may be created to carry road traffic over railroad tracks or other highways. There are even bridges built specifically for trains, and those only built to carry pipelines for oil and gases. These types of bridges are called viaducts.

In big cities where skyscrapers are common, bridges may be built connecting two buildings together. These skywalks allow people to travel from building to building without having to cross over busy streets or highways. Whether a bridge is man-made or natural, one thing is for certain: getting around would be a much more difficult task without them. And as the world's population grows, engineers will need to find ways to build longer and stronger bridges to help keep people moving.

Suspension bridge in Indonesia

INDEX

Skytrain Bridge in Greater Vancouver, B.C.

DATE DUE			
Bosco			
FEB 2 7 2009			
0 1 2009			